TEN LOW-
STARTUP ID
DITCH Y

MW01065483

EVERY BRAND HAS AN ORIGIN STORY.

OUR JOB IS TO HELP YOU CREATE YOURS.

PEOPLE ARE A LOT MORE CREATIVE AND ENTREPRENEURIAL THAN THEY REALIZE.

THE IDEA AND TASK OF LAUNCHING SOMETHING FROM SCRATCH IS DAUNTING AND OVERWHELMING. WHERE TO EVEN BEGIN?

WE WRESTLE WITH UNCERTAINTY, SELF-DOUBT, AND ARE UNSURE WHERE AND HOW TO EVEN BEGIN.

WE'RE HERE TO HELP.

WHAT WE'RE ABOUT

HELPING YOU LAUNCH STARTUPS
SO YOU CAN ENJOY THE FREEDOM
OF DOING SOMETHING THAT
YOU'RE GOOD AT, INTERESTED IN,
AND PASSIONATE ABOUT.

TEN LOW-COST / NO-COST STARTUP IDEAS TO HELP YOU DITCH YOUR DAY JOB

Published by URTHTREK, LLC.

URTHTREK, LLC
2034 NE 40th Ave. #414
Portland, OR 97212

urthtrek.com
@urthtrek

Manufactured in the United States of America.

ISBN: 978-0-578-26578-0

All photos and design are from Unsplash.com or by the author. Design and typesetting by the author.

CONTENTS

INTRODUCTION   1

CHAPTER 1   7
Photography

CHAPTER 2   15
Social Media Management

CHAPTER 3   23
Self-Publishing

CHAPTER 4   31
Roasting Coffee or Baking

CHAPTER 5   39
Be an Expert / Coaching

CHAPTER 6   47
Building Websites

CHAPTER 7   55
Start a Magazine

CHAPTER 8   63
Create a Non-Profit

CHAPTER 9   **71**
Content Matter Expert

CHAPTER 10   **79**
Product Reviewer

WRAP-UP   **87**

    About the Author   91
    About Startup Coaching   95
    About URTHTREK   99

INTRODUCTION

I hear it regularly. It's why people sign up for the startup coaching I offer. They want a new job. A new career. Somewhere along the way, the career path they had chosen either isn't as meaningful and fulfilling as they had assumed. Or, maybe they hit a dead-end at their job. They've hit the ceiling. For some, it's the realization they don't want to be office-bound. Going through the pandemic gave many a taste of working from home or on the road. There's no turning back.

Regardless of the motives, there's a drive and eagerness to try something new. It could have something to do with previous schooling and degrees or be a complete pivot. While many who come through our startup coaching know what they want to start, others are uneasy because of a lack of clarity about startup ideas.

That's why I wrote this guide. To give you a few ideas to get your creative juices flowing. I would classify most people who come through our startup coaching as makers or artisans. They are building or creating something ... coffee, vegan bread, tattoos, gluten-free muffins, photos, websites, and more. Or, they're offering services ... personal training, coaching, brand consulting, adventure guiding, and more. But for the rest? It can be stressful.

But don't stress! The good news is the startup idea you land on probably won't be your last. Or, once you begin down the road of starting, you will inevitably pivot. But don't let this cause you even more anxiety. It's all part of the fun and adventure. As much as we try and dispel all of the ambiguity in starting something from scratch, there's no way to get rid of it all.

Almost every startup pivots. Netflix used to mail DVDs to your home. We used to get all of our news a day late delivered to our doorsteps in weird rolled papers (newspapers). The key is to start. To get your idea and activities in motion. As the saying goes, it's easier to steer a boat once it's left harbor rather than when it's tied to the dock.

Let's set your boat free. It's time to push off and set sail.

With that said, I want to share with you ten low-cost or no-cost startup ideas to get you started. This list is by no way exhaustive. These are also ideas based on what I hear people are interested in creating and what is required to get going. It also reflects popular startup ideas among those we've worked with and continue to coach. While it's rare to start a business where the next day it goes viral and you're able to ditch your day job, this will at least begin moving you in that direction. Are you ready? Let's go!

CHAPTER 1
PHOTOGRAPHY

With every idea I share, our first response is, "Who, me?" "No way, that market is saturated." Or is it?

What person or brand doesn't need quality photography? As we've become a digital or social media-centric society, that means the importance of quality photography only elevates. Sure, the latest iPhone captures impressive images, but it's still an iPhone.

When I first started my coffee roasting company seven years ago, all I had was an iPhone. Back then, I was still a few iPhone generations behind from the latest and greatest (I still am). But since that was all I had, I used it to snap photos for social media. To say our social media presence was lackluster was an understatement. But since it was the Wild West of Instagram, it didn't prevent us from growing rapidly. But over time, things began to change.

Through social media, I had connected with several professional photographers. We set up a fun bartering service … coffee for photos. They were often on the run, traveling, and the thought of having free coffee was appealing. For me, I wanted and needed quality photos that: (a) weren't taken with my iPhone 4, (b) were high quality to use for social media and our website, and (c) was of scenery and people not in and around Portland.

Soon I was getting photos from all over the world … the Alps, Norway, South Africa,

Whistler, Lake Tahoe, and more. It was amazing. Quality photography completely elevated our brand. When magazines reached out to do articles on us, I could supply amazing photos to go with them.

Quality photography matters. A lot. So why not start a business around it?

There are a million ideas of what you can also specialize in … portraits, products (coffee, whiskey, flowers, etc.), motorcycles, sports (basketball, football, soccer, etc.), the outdoors, van life, and anything and everything that you can take a photo of. You see, it's more than blindly jumping into photography, but you can craft a business around hobbies and activities you're interested in and passionate about.

Not only that, but it doesn't have to cost you a fortune. If you're hunting for a good camera, especially if you look at full-frame mirrorless ones, it does come with sticker shock. But you don't have to start there.

Last year I taught an undergrad course called Social Media and Analytics. I already knew a student in my class, Marcos, because he took Interpersonal Communications from me the previous year as a freshman. He's an aspiring entrepreneur and had started a protein bar company with his friend … as a freshman. We talked a lot about social media (obviously), which got us talking about photography. He wanted to take his energy bar brand to the next level, but all he had was an iPhone. He asked about getting a digital camera. We talked, he told me his budget, and I shot him the name of a camera he could snag for that price.

With a budget of around $250-$300, I suggested he pick up a Canon T3i. It's a great starter camera, and with good lighting, it can snap some fantastic photos. He found one on eBay with a lens. I also loaned him my 50mm lens. To say it opened a whole new world for him would be an understatement. He picked up the camera by the end of the Spring semester. He spent all summer practicing taking photos and learning editing in Lightroom. We'd meet up for a coffee, talk, walk, and take pictures together.

By the end of the summer, he was smitten. He created a new Instagram page and website and began freelancing as a photographer, specializing in portraits. His friends were lining up to have him take their photos. I also had Marcos in class this past fall. We would talk about photography lots. Towards the end of the semester, he made the jump up to a full-frame mirrorless camera. Marcos was on his way!

What was his starting point? Less than $300 on an older Canon T3i. That's all he needed. Sure, if you have a higher-end camera with quality glass, you know you can spot the difference, but for most everyone else? They can't tell. That's why I like to include photography as a low-cost / no-cost startup idea. It doesn't cost much.

When I got a camera for my coffee roasting company, it was a Canon T3 (not even a T3i). $225 on eBay. That lasted a year until I found a Canon 5D Mark II on eBay for $400. I bought a couple of EF lenses (24-70mm and 70-200mm) and was off and running before transitioning to a full-frame mirrorless myself. The point? I was stoked on my photos each step of the way. I even took pictures on my lowly Canon T3, which landed in well-known companies' ads and articles. No one knew but me the camera they were taken on.

The good news is you CAN do this! Start small (if you want) and level up from there. Since it's low-cost, what do you have to lose?

The question then is … where do you start? One easy way is to throw out on social media that you're doing free photoshoots and to DM you if someone is interested. What inevitably happens is not only do people start reaching out to you, but most won't even let you do it for free. They will insist on paying you at least something. Guess what? You're well on your way.

Obviously, that's an oversimplification. However, you have to start somewhere. Maybe what you need most is repetition in the beginning. You also get your name out there. News spreads fast. Along the way, you'll naturally begin taking other steps without thinking about it ... new social media accounts specifically for your photography business and a website. The point? Start simple, start small, and level up from there.

CHAPTER 2

SOCIAL MEDIA MANAGEMENT

We live in the digital age. That does not mean industries like agriculture, manufacturing, and the like are gone or unimportant. It simply means because of technological advancements, whole new industries and careers continue to come ... well, online.

Speaking of agriculture. Just because you're a farmer, rancher, or run a landscaping business, it doesn't mean having an online presence is unimportant. In fact, it's more important than ever before. To make ends meet while in college, my brother-in-law began mowing lawns. Fast forward the storyline, and he runs a very successful lawn care business specializing in eco-friendly premium products that make peoples' yards magazine-worthy.

He grew up on a farm and is a man of the land, yet so much of what we talk about is social media and digital marketing. Too often, we talk about these kinds of things and assume it's only for fashion brands, influencers, and tech companies. Instead, it's trickled down to everyone. As a matter of fact, the last conversation I had with my brother-in-law was about him looking to hire a digital marketing agency.

Social media management is not only a viable low-cost / no-cost startup idea, but as far as the who, it could delve into any industry you're passionate about! There are no limits (except in our own minds). Who doesn't need a growing social media platform? Also, many who start and lead companies either (a) don't have the time to run social media or (b) it's not in their wheelhouse of expertise.

You might be surprised by the kinds of conversations I've had with people in need of someone running their social media. Some of these are companies I would deem as having very strong and well-defined brands. Not only that, but their content is top-notch. But when you start looking, you realize they may post 2-3 times a month and only get around to sending out newsletters once in a while. In other words, there's a HUGE need for social media management (along with email newsletter campaigns).

Keep in mind there are varying layers or levels to this. It could be as simple as posting content that is fed your way where all you're doing is posting and managing. At the other end of the spectrum, you're the one out there taking photos and even creating videos, developing content strategies, and more. Then there's everything in between. While I understand that this idea of a "social media manager" might be laughable to some, it's actually such an essential part of a brand. In fact, most often, it is the front door into the brand.

You know, and I know, that whenever we come across a new brand, we immediately look for them on social media. Most often on Instagram. Without anyone telling us anything, we intuitively learn almost everything we need to know about their brand by simply glancing at their feed. Are the images high quality and attractive? How often do they post? Again, without anyone saying anything to us, we'll either dive deeper or jump off their page within only a few seconds. Their brand is either appealing or repelling. Off-putting. We gather that all in a few seconds.

Social media matters. It's also a viable business to get into. To manage either one or a variety of accounts. You're taking an enormous burden off someone's shoulder, and in return, you're creating peace and excitement by consistently creating and posting top-notch content. That most often includes photos and copy (words).

As far as the startup costs? Usually, it begins with a computer, preferably a laptop. I'm assuming you already have one. On top of that, if you provide other services such as photography, well, I just covered that in the last section. So, in the end, what would it cost to get into social media management? Time and a lot of determination.

The question you may have for this idea and all the others is, where do you even start? Most often, it's about relationships and networks. Talk to friends and other people you know. Offer to do a test run for someone or start off small.

In one of the accounts we manage, we only post half the month along with writing a couple articles and sending one newsletter. For another, it's almost daily posts, articles, coordinating communication, and photography. For another, it's more focused on 1-2 email newsletters a month, an occasional post on Facebook, and working on getting them on some more platforms. There's a wide variety.

As I've shared, most often, this allows you to work remotely. That doesn't necessarily mean you'll be parked along some unnamed beach on the Baja peninsula in Mexico for months at a time, but you're definitely not checking into an office. You can work from home, coffee shops, and yes, even on the road. That depends on your arrangement with the companies you're managing the social media for. Sometimes you need to be closer to home and accessible; other times, there are gaps where you can take off and explore while you manage their social media from afar.

People and companies need social media help, so why not create a new business for yourself around social media management?

CHAPTER 3
SELF-PUBLISHING

My first startup was actually a publishing company. I had no idea what I was doing other than knowing how to write, I loved writing, and I had a lot of friends with PhDs who were itching to turn their dissertations into books. Add a bit of creativity to that, and I was off and running.

Well, more like stumbling. And stumble I did. But sure enough, I started to ramp up the number of books we were publishing a year.

Some books won awards. Others could be found in the libraries of Cal Berkley, Stanford, Ivy League schools, and other universities worldwide.

I'll never forget one time when I was at my gym and received a phone call. I usually don't answer, but I did. I was a bit out of breath. On the other end of the phone was a bookstore manager from a university in Australia. They were calling about getting one of our books into their campus bookstore. She was shocked when I answered the phone with a simple, "Hello?" (Unfortunately, with heavy breathing too.)

The bookstore manager assumed we were some massive publishing company with layers of people doing all sorts of things ... like answering the phone. Instead, it was me ... the founder, president / CEO, graphic designer, typesetter, website designer, and social media manager all wrapped up in one sweaty out-of-breath dude in the gym. And we grew.

After a few years, I realized it wasn't my life's dream and ambition to run a more academic-focused publishing company. Instead, I sold it to three professor friends and simultaneously launched my coffee roasting company. It was a great three-year run; I learned lots and am still publishing books (my own). It's a blast.

Changing technologies have had a transformative impact on so many industries. For me, it all came into focus and validity when a few years ago, Chance the Rapper won all kinds of music awards. What was unusual was he didn't sign with a record label. He did it on his own. With such platforms as Spotify and YouTube, why bother? The same is true with publishing.

It used to be that the publishing companies acted as guardians. Like giant sentinels standing at the gate of the publishing world, they would determine who would get it … and who wouldn't (which was most). After several years in this world, I realized that authors often got published because either (a) they knew someone or had a connection within a publishing company, or (b) they were a big deal.

It was at this time that I started learning about print-on-demand technology. I didn't need my own printer nor a warehouse full of books on pallets I desperately hoped to sell. Print-on-demand meant I didn't need the overhead of a printer or the space. All I needed was my computer. I used to walk across the street to our neighborhood McDonald's, sip on bad $1 coffee, and work on my new publishing company. Like Chance the Rapper, I learned I could forgo the big-name publishers … the sentinels … and instead bring my own ideas and books to market (even like I am today with this book).

So much has changed since then, but the premise is still valid. You can still start your own publishing company with nothing more than a laptop. Heck, you don't even need to create your own whole company. Instead, this could be your avenue to bring your own thoughts, ideas, and creativity into print and sell on all the major platforms globally.

Lately, I've been fascinated with all-things #vanlife. That's because last fall I bought a 1995 Chevy Sport Van … aka, Nacho. Nacho even has his own Instagram (@nachothevan). While I don't intend to live full-time in Nacho, a few days here, a few weeks there is what I'm working towards. Plus, there's a lot of fantastic scenery between Portland (where I live) and northern Arizona, where my Mom lives.

As a result, I've picked up a few books on Amazon about van-living … how to do it, ditch your day job, and other things to keep in mind. Reading this book in the evenings has become super fun as my day is winding down. From the get-go, I knew and could tell that one of the authors I'm reading is self-publishing her books. She's a full-time van lifer. What a creative way to earn residual income! Write a book … or several books … edit the manuscripts, design the cover, typeset, and then through print-on-demand technologies (and Kindle), upload your books for the world to read!

The good news, all you need is a laptop computer, creativity, a willingness to learn and make mistakes, and you can not only self-publish your own books but work towards starting your own publishing company. You get to focus on whatever genre piques your interest and curiosity. That's why I've included it as a low-cost / no-cost startup idea.

The best way to start is with an experiment, your own book. Write it, get it copyedited (whether yourself, a friend, or even a program like Grammarly), design the cover, typeset the interior, and upload it to whatever print-on-demand company you choose. I used KDP, or Kindle Direct Publishing, the print-on-demand platform through Amazon. Why? Because when your book goes live, it is distributed globally through their channels.

Beyond that, all you need then is to build your website, set up your social media, and you're off and running. Yes, it really could be as simple as that. Obviously, it helps to have some kind of strategy or plan, but since it's low-cost / no-cost, you can build this as you go.

CHAPTER 4

ROASTING COFFEE OR BAKING

With any startup idea, you can place them on a continuum. Specifically, you can create its own continuum or spectrum for each one. At one end is what it'd take to get this idea off the ground with everything fully built out. On the other end, it's more about the least amount you need to get started. Usually, then everything else falls somewhere in between.

Take coffee, for example. There's an enormous disparity between having a built-out roasting facility with one or multiple roasters where you can roast 200-500-1,000+ pounds a week versus serving pourover coffees out of your existing van. Both are in the "coffee industry." Speaking of serving coffee out of a van, that's what I started building for fun. Let me explain.

As I shared before, I used to have a coffee roasting company—more about that in a moment. But what I would like to share is not only about my van Nacho, but a spontaneous a-ha moment I had to create a new business with it. It's using Nacho to cater or serve coffee at trailheads and outdoor events. Now let's add up the costs …

I already had the van. Truth be told, I paid $200 for it. So what would it take or cost to set it up as a mobile coffee van? I had to buy gas burners, scales, pourover set-ups (drippers and carafes), a portable electric generator, a coffee grinder, a couple of kettles, etc. Beyond that, I purchased small tables and a stool to brew coffee inside my van (it rains a lot in the PNW). I also needed a retractable awning. All said, even with buying Nacho, I spent below $1,000.

While it's not no-cost, it's close. To do an event serving coffee, I can charge anywhere between $350-$1,000. Within 1-2 events, guess what? It's already paid for. Not only that, but I have a way to keep paying for upgrades for Nacho, which I can also write off as a business expense.

Now let's talk coffee roasting. On the one hand, you can go all-in and drop $25,000 on a 6kg roaster and several more thousands to get your roasting facility up and going … green beans, buckets, bags, chaff burner, bag sealer, scales, and more. Or, find a roaster and have them do a white label set-up for you. In other words, they roast for you, bag for you, apply your label, and ship for you. Then you split the profits accordingly. All you need to do is set up a website and socials and market like crazy. That is 100% how I stumbled into coffee roasting.

My goal was to launch a mountain bike guiding company initially. After a failed crowdfunding campaign, I was a bit discouraged. I had a friend reach out to me to tell me that he knew someone who could roast coffee for me to sell as a fundraiser. We'd split the profits 50-50. I needed to come up with a name, design a label, and poof! I'm in!

So that's what I did. I created a name as well as a website. It made sense also to create social media accounts so I could spread the word. Just like that, I started. Zero upfront costs. I take that back; I spent $10 a month on a Squarespace website. But guess what happened? It began to grow—a lot.

Within the first year, we steadily gained traction on social media and in sales. We were featured in a couple of magazines. After the first year, I realized I might have stumbled onto something. At that point, I bought a roaster and began learning how to roast. After another six months, I went completely out on my own. I was a coffee roaster in the coffee industry from that point forward. I learned everything on the fly and had a blast while making many mistakes. But I learned a lot along the way.

Today, the bar to entry is relatively low, whether through white labeling or access to shared roasters that you can rent by the hour. I've seen roaster after roaster in Portland get their start on the same shared roaster. Eventually, some outgrow it, buy their own roaster, and get their own space. But to start there (fully built-out) would be prohibitive for most.

I add baking into this because it runs on parallel tracks as far as getting going. Like coffee, there are shared commercial kitchens to get started. I have a friend who's starting a vegan bakery. Long before moving into a space that is currently getting built out, he started small and nimble. He began with a weekly bread subscription delivered to your door. All it takes is one subscription, then two, then four, then ten, and suddenly, you have a growing customer base and income stream. While this and coffee are not conducive to living on the road in a van, it's a good entry point for those who're more stationary.

As I've shared repeatedly, you can get in with almost no money with coffee and baking. Whether you want to roast coffee yourself, sell through a white label partnership, or serve it with a coffee cart, there are plenty of entry points—the same with baking. If you're interested, begin looking around locally or regionally for shared spaces and white label opportunities, and start the conversations. While you may start small, it doesn't mean that you won't have your own full-on roaster or bakery someday soon. Start small, but start somewhere.

CHAPTER 5

BE AN EXPERT / COACHING

Just this morning, I had a conversation about coaching … in one of my coaching calls. Weird. But maybe you don't know why it was or is funny. It's that term. Coaching. It's kind of like the words entrepreneur or startup. As soon as one of those words is uttered, we're suddenly swept away with perceptions and misconceptions that pack those words so full of meaning.

One of the topics we talk about in my startup coaching is those words. We get hung up on them. "Who me? An entrepreneur?" "I can't launch a startup." We assume entrepreneurs all have to be Type-A hype beasts or that startups require millions of dollars raised through angel investors. We also stumble over the word "coaching."

My conversation this morning was with an African American leader who does extensive work in his East coast city and within the Black community. As we meet every other week, the startup idea he's building has evolved into coaching. Today, he finally realized that. No, he knew what he was doing and creating, but he, like me, was hung up on that word "coaching."

I see all kinds of ads, and we all have friends who are Life Coaches, Executive Coaches, etc. Many spent hundreds of hours (if not more) getting all of the proper certifications to aid them in their business and provide a baseline level of credentials for coaching. Many (most?) assume that it is needed to be a coach or do coaching. After talking with my friend this morning, the revelation was that what he is doing is indeed coaching. Plain and simple. He came to grips with what it was.

Listen, we all struggle with imposter syndrome. I was 1/3 of the way working towards my second doctorate, a Ph.D. in Urban Studies, before I took a pause. I was almost a double-Dr. Do you think any labels (Dr.) are a repellent of imposter syndrome? Not remotely. I struggled with it. Honestly, I still do.

When I first began startup coaching, I tried to be all coy about it. I called them "cohorts"... because obviously, that makes sense and everyone knows what that is. After having to explain over and over and over ... and over again, what a cohort was or is, it dawned on me I was trying to outthink the room. The service I was offering was simple. Startup coaching. I help coach people to start businesses and non-profits. Once I changed the language, people suddenly knew what I had offered.

I coach. My friend is coaching minority leaders to lead businesses, non-profits, and churches. So what is coaching, and why is it shrouded in not only mystery, but it also gives off Illuminati vibes? Not only that, but why am I putting it in this list of low-cost / no-cost startup ideas?

Everyone is a specialist in something. Everyone. You are somebody. You have something to offer ... a skill, wisdom, insight, experience, know-how, and more. Coaching is simply helping people learn to do this. Yes, there's already pushback. I can feel it, especially from the non-directive coaching crowd.

For several years a while back, I was involved in a coaching relationship. I connected with someone who coached for a living, and he took me on. I hated it. A lot. It was two years of non-directive coaching. What is non-directive coaching? I found this description online, "In non-directive coaching, the individual or group is the expert, and they set the agenda. The coach helps them to think through that agenda

and then apply their own expertise to achieve
the outcomes they want." I wasn't interested in
someone trying to extract answers, decisions,
or solutions out of me that were supposedly
already there. I wanted new information. New
insights. New knowledge. A new set of skills.

I know so much coaching is non-directive, and
it drives me crazy (sorry if I offended you). I
don't do that kind of coaching. My friend
Charlie doesn't do that kind of coaching.
People are coming to me … to Charlie …
because they need help doing something,
navigating new terrain, and more. As a result, I
have a curriculum that I walk people through
over ten months. I even call it a syllabus since
my professor's brain is always in that mode.

I've learned that I can be myself and coach in a
way that's akin to who I am. You can coach as
well. What skill or expertise could you offer? I
think of some of my friends and the coaching
businesses they could start … Sam can show
you how to create a fantastic brand as well as
your own magazine. Jerel can teach you how to

raise money as he's raised millions of dollars for non-profits. Brian can help you start a specialty coffee roastery in a rural community. Matt can walk you through how to create a tattoo business from scratch. Andy can teach you how to start a high-end custom furniture company.

Because of technology, the good news is that you can do this anywhere. Any place you can get wifi or cellular reception. I do everything on Zoom ... because I have slides to share like a professor. Talk about #vanlife compatible! The biggest hurdle or obstacle is usually within us. You have something to share. You're an expert in some area or field or industry. There are people out there who would not only benefit from your coaching and mentoring them but would be willing to pay you.

So how do you start? As with most things, we begin with a website, create social media accounts, and then spread the word among friends and family. It's how many startups are launched. Then we go from there, develop strategies related to branding and marketing, and we're off to the races!

Why not you?

CHAPTER 6

BUILDING WEBSITES

Last semester I taught an undergrad course called Introduction to Web Design. Interestingly, the course was less about coding and more about the design and functionality of websites. In fact, no coding was involved. Instead, we spent the semester analyzing, test-driving, and talking through what makes a website work.

Each Monday in class, I'd share with the students three different websites. At their desks, they'd pull up these websites on their computers, one at a time, and peruse through them. Did the websites make sense? Were they self-evident? Was it easy or difficult to navigate? Could the students even figure out what the website was about, what the company was selling or offering, and how to purchase or sign up? I love university students because they don't hold back with their critiques. In a fun way, it became a weekly roasting session.

To be fair, I intentionally put myself and some of my own websites in the line of fire. I think I gave my students a little too much freedom to roast me and my websites. They dropped their proverbial boxer's gloves, and bare-knuckled punched my websites. We had a blast, and it was a fun learning experience.

Truth be told, one of the first websites I shared with them was my very own URTHTREK website. I've spent countless hours building and refining … and refining … and improving … and refining. I intended to share a website with the students that was done well. You know, as a template. I couldn't have been more wrong. After ten minutes of perusing my website, we debriefed it as a class. They were lost.

What was my website even about? What did I do? What is URTHTREK even about? One student thought I was offering counseling services. Another determined I was a personal trainer. The verdict? They didn't know what it was about nor what I did or was offering.

Needless to say, it was a humbling experience. Here I was, a professor teaching web design, and one of my own websites didn't make sense or was clear. I realized quickly that I had put a little too much emphasis on design and layout rather than making it clear, including my offerings and call-to-actions. Throughout the semester, we did this over and over again. We looked at all sorts of brands, from major popular ones we all know all of the way down to local startups.

One of my encouragements to these students was that they actually knew enough to build their own website and do so for hire by the end of the semester. No, you don't need to know coding. I'm not saying that's unimportant at all, but with the various tools and website builders out there, you can not only build beautiful websites, but others will pay you to do so.

It was a no-brainer for me to include building websites when it comes to low-cost / no-cost startup or side hustle ideas. With anything, there are varying degrees. There's an enormous difference in complexity in websites ranging from airlines to your friend who is starting a mobile florist. Think of all of the startups we know and the friends we have who are launching them ... dog walking, coffee roasting, tattoos, food carts, personal training, coaching, consulting, real estate, and more. You can provide significant value by building quality, aesthetically appealing, and affordable websites.

While I'm painting the picture that you … yes, you … can actually do this, it also comes with a steep learning curve. Building websites is both an art and a science. It helps to be creative and have an eye for design. One of the things you'll learn over time, whether we're talking photography, painting, baking, or in this case, web design, you will find and develop your own style. I know my websites all have a similar "vibe" to them. Why? I have my own style. Over time people will identify you by your style and then hire you specifically for that look.

So how do you get started?

I would recommend finding a friend who needs a website built. Tell them you'll create it for free. Then have them sign up for Squarespace (or Wix, Square, GoDaddy, etc.) and share the log-in credentials with you. Once you log in, you're off to the races!

Is it really that simple?

No, but I at least wanted to make it as easy as possible to get started. Besides, that's actually how a lot of people start. For me, it wasn't building websites for others but for my own. I always have startup ideas bouncing around in my head. As I'm getting these ideas off the ground, it means building a website. I have free ones all of the way to paid ones. The key is to practice and build up your skill and competency.

While I laid out an over-the-top simplistic way to start, what that does is provide a basic structure. Then, over time, you'll find yourself filling it in with more details, steps, and processes. For example, whenever I build a website for a client, I send them a survey to fill out. It helps me gather information. No, not info to fill out each page on the website with, but what I'm trying to discover is what "vibe" or "look" they want for their website. Along the way, we talk about their target audience, design considerations, what their website is about, and even other websites they love and are inspired by.

My goal in this chapter is not as much to walk you through how to make this a way to earn income but to let you know that it is indeed a viable option. In other words, you can do this. I've already had students who've started building websites for their friends (or other professors). Most often, that's how it starts. Along the way, you may want to add to your credentials and certifications, but until then, most everything you need to know is on YouTube.

You got this. You can do it. And yes, people will pay you to build them a website.

CHAPTER 7

START A MAGAZINE

For those of us who grew up before the digital age, we've been forever shaped by the esteemed place of magazines in our lives. Wait, did that just make me sound really old? Growing up, I think of the moment when I'd pick up a magazine. Maybe it was a heavy metal magazine in junior high or Rolling Stone, but there was something special about them.

Truth be told, I didn't pay much attention to who the writers were or all of the ads. In fact, I never put much thought into what it even took to produce a magazine. All I knew was I'd read interviews of my favorite bands or athletes and was entertained. The photography was also top-notch.

So why would I recommend you start a magazine?

It's like anything we've explored thus far, there's perception, and then there's reality. It's like the chapter on self-publishing or starting a publishing company. There's a perception of how books are created and distributed. And then there's the reality. I'd much rather live in a world of reality than myths and perceptions. Those usually are false.

Perception: you need to publish a book through a traditional publisher to be a best-selling author. Reality: you can self-publish your own book and be a best-selling author. Perception: only big agencies have the money, people power, and infrastructure to produce a high-quality magazine. Reality: you can produce your own high-quality magazine.

One of the recurring themes in this book is about changing and advancing technologies. This allows access and opportunity for anyone to create and distribute their own content, whether books, magazines, music, and more. So why did I include magazines as an option for a low-cost / no-cost startup idea? Well, because it fits. Not only that but scaling up can bring about tremendous opportunities and even income. There, I said it. Like anything, it has the potential to become lucrative.

When I had my coffee roasting company that catered to mountain bikers, I'd get hit up to buy ads in various mountain bike magazines and prominent media websites. Along with their proposal email, they'd send over a pitch deck. The idea behind their pitch deck was to show me who their readers were, how many magazines were sold, their reach, rate of growth over the previous year, and more. Then when they hit you with the crazy price tag for a

1/4 page ad, I'm supposed to think it was a great deal. I'm sure it was, but I declined every time.

One time I added up how much this particular magazine would pull in for ads for each issue. I'm no math expert, but it was somewhere between $50,000-$100,000 per issue. On top of that, people still have to drop over $10 to buy the magazine. I think the last I checked, they had over 60,000 in distribution. Do a little math, and … ok, maybe this isn't such a bad startup idea at all!

My friend Sam started a magazine on a whim. He owns and runs Kids & Cobras, a moto-inspired coffee roasting company in Portland. He decided one day to launch a magazine. It's called the *Slow Mag*. The best part? He had never done this before, nor wasn't too sure how to even start. So he created and designed the magazine on his computer using InDesign. He knew of a local printer and emailed the file to them. And just like that, he was off and running.

Like anything, we learn along the way. So is Sam. Why did he start the Slow Mag? He loves telling stories and wanted a different complementary platform to tell stories from the moto community. In the magazine, coffee articles are mixed with stories of various people within the moto community. Add to that top-notch photography, and he has a beautiful magazine.

My question to you is … why not you? What kind of magazine would you want to start? What would your theme or focus be? The way to answer that is to ask what you're passionate about. What interests you? Sam is passionate about coffee and moto culture. What about you?

Like anything, the key is you can start small and grow from there. It doesn't cost you anything other than time to design a magazine. Sure, there are printing costs … $4-$7 per magazine. If you sell them for $10 each, you can already see your profit margin. That's not even including paid ads. As your magazine grows, along with its reach and readership, there will be brands interested in advertising. You just may get enough paid ad content to more than cover all of your printing costs. At that point, everything on top of that is profit. Again, there are many variables, but now you can at least see how you could do this and get going.

For some of you, you may want to forgo a printed magazine altogether and create a digital one. The same premise, but you're not having to deal with printing costs. But as you can see, this is definitely a low-cost / no-cost startup idea. What are you waiting for?

Interestingly, I've been kicking around this idea for a while myself too. I've since learned to ask the question, "why not?" instead of "why?" Through talking with Sam and writing this chapter, I decided to jump in and give this a whirl myself. If you haven't figured it out by now, I love starting things. I've also learned that I'm good at it. Lastly, I know I can create something that people want to buy, including the companies themselves. That's why I sold the last two startups I started.

Over the last 48 hours, I finally landed on my magazine idea and name. Since then, I've set up everything on social media, bought the domain name, and hired someone to design my logo. I've started creating a road map to releasing my first magazine edition in six months. What's my theme for my first edition? What stories do I want to tell? How will I design it? What will my "look" or "vibe" be? Will I do print only? Print and digital? What about paid ads?

The truth is, at this moment in time, I don't know. But the exciting part is developing a plan, creating a brand identity, and moving through the steps to go from idea to launch. You can start a magazine too.

CHAPTER 8

CREATE A
NON-PROFIT

What breaks your heart? What are you concerned about? What justice or advocacy issues light the flames of your passions? You may want to consider launching a non-profit startup to address a need.

The follow-up question is, why a non-profit and not a "common good" for-profit business? Great question. What can you do through a non-profit that you couldn't do through a regular company? While there are pros and cons for approaches to both, when it comes to addressing injustices or issues of advocacy, then going the non-profit route is a great way to go.

Truth be told, I've started a few non-profits myself. Each had its own reasoning behind them. What makes them unique, most often, then is the business model. In other words, how is income generated? Obviously, the lines blur for sure, especially when we broach the topic of a social enterprise. A social enterprise or social business is defined as a business with specific social objectives that serve its primary purpose. Social enterprises seek to maximize profits while maximizing benefits to society and the environment.

You now see then that sometimes what separates non-profits from for-profits could be somewhat of a razor-thin fictitious line. Obviously, how they are registered with the state and other things play a role. So why am I suggesting you start a non-profit?

Before I got into business startups, I was involved exclusively in the non-profit world. As I shared, I even started a couple of them myself. Also, I currently still run one as well. But first of all, let's talk about mountain biking and trails.

Since last fall, I've been working as the Communications Director for the Northwest Trail Alliance (NWTA). We are a volunteer-led non-profit that creates, enhances, and protects mountain bike opportunities in Northwest Oregon and Southwest Washington. Our mission is to advocate for new trails, protect, improve, and build sustainable mountain bike trails, and create recreation opportunities for mountain biking. My role consists of photography, coordinating social media, and the like. I get to tell stories of volunteers who build and maintain our regional trails.

We have around 6,000 members and are led by an all-volunteer board of directors. Collectively, they'll put in hundreds of hours a year leading the NWTA. On top of that, they too volunteer by grabbing a shovel or McCleod and getting dirty building trails. As a volunteer organization, we generate income by paid membership. That, on top of the various grants we apply for and partnerships (or sponsorships) with for-profit businesses, is what funds us to do what we need to do. We buy and maintain equipment, at times subcontract with trail building companies on specific projects, and everything else that comes with maintaining countless miles of mountain biking trails in our region.

We have a unique place and voice as a non-profit and volunteer group. As a result, we partner with our local city government. Last fall, for example, we entered into a formal partnership with the Bureau of Land Management (BLM) to be the trail stewards of a trail system on the western flank of Mt Hood.

We also have an advocacy director who, again, is a volunteer. He is the one working closely with the local government. When needed, he mobilizes our membership to show up for local city meetings or contact various government leaders to let our voices be known about specific projects.

Could we do this as a for-profit business? I'm sure we could. But our goal isn't profit. I vividly recall showing up for our last annual meeting. Because of COVID, we hadn't met in person for almost two years. On a Sunday afternoon, over sixty of us gathered at Chris King HQ to meet. It was a day of celebration. One by one, we heard people share as to why they're not only at that meeting but are involved in trail stewardship. These are people who give away countless weekends a year to dig. Why? Because they're passionate about this issue. It hit me that this was a room of sixty volunteers.

As a non-profit, it doesn't mean there's no paid staff. I'm paid part-time, and we have a part-time Executive Director. We're in the process of hiring a full-time Executive Director. I also sit on the board of two other non-profits. They, too, have paid staff. Each organization has its own focus or reason for being.

What would your reason be for starting a non-profit? What are you interested in and passionate about? For me, it's mountain biking all the way. If I lived elsewhere, I'd for sure start up my own non-profit trail organization. Or least become a chapter of a large national organization. Why? There's just a lot you can do as a non-profit, including accessing certain buckets of funding. Also, your bottom line is different. Your bottom line isn't strictly about financial gain. Obviously, you need income to sustain yourself and your organization's mission.

I'm a massive fan of this option for thinking through startups. They, too, can be low-cost or no-cost. Depending on your services, you will probably have almost no overhead or expenses right away. If you were to launch a non-profit, what would you start? What need, pain point, or justice issue do you want to address with your non-profit?

Obviously, this is not a how-to book on all of the steps needed to start a for-profit business or non-profit organization. While the processes are nearly identical to both, again, one of the biggest differentiators will be how you generate income so you can address whatever objectives or pain points you're passionate about. What needs do you want to meet or address?

CHAPTER 9

CONTENT MATTER
EXPERT

What are you good at? More so, in what areas are you moving to become an "expert?" Now, before you answer, first of all, you'll need to un-invite an unwelcome guest who's occupying too much space in your brain. Who's this intruder, you might ask? We can call them "imposter syndrome."

Who? Me? An expert? Hopefully, you don't cough milk out of your nose when I told you that you really are an expert ... because you are. Each of us has something of value that we can bring to the world. And yes, we quickly dismiss that statement as our imposter syndrome not only rudely plops onto the couch in our midst but has the audacity to kick their feet up on our coffee table. How rude!

I have a theory I've been working on and mulling over. It goes like this ... regardless of age, those who can remove the doubt of imposter syndrome are those who not only begin making progress towards realizing their dreams but, in the end, become successful. What that means is most often, the greatest obstacle is from within. Us.

So once we un-invite the imposter syndrome, then let's circle back around to the question I asked at the beginning of this chapter ... what are you good at? Not only that but in what areas are you an expert? We all have something of value that we can bring and contribute. We have insight, knowledge, know-how, and there are not only many who want to hear it but would even be willing to pay you for it. I know, it almost sounds too good to be true, right?

It's not.

This kind of scenario is not uncommon in higher education. Besides, you got to school to become a subject matter or content expert. You end up doing research and writing a dissertation on some obscure random topic that makes you an expert. But you don't need to go to grad school (or even undergrad) to be an expert in something. The question becomes then, not only what are you an expert in (or burgeoning expert), but how can you maximize that and turn it into a business?

I vividly remember working hard to get my coffee roasting business off the ground. I was having a blast and making plenty of mistakes along the way. For the first several years, I never took any income from it. It all went back into the business. I worked full-time elsewhere anyway, so I could do that as I built things up.

During this time, I'd get invited to speak on my professor's side of life from time to time. One time, in particular, stood out. I lead a one-day workshop up in Seattle. The host organization paid for my rental car and gas and my hotel and meals. On top of that, I was paid to speak. It was a blast, and I love doing this. As I drove home and reflected on it, I realized I made more money at that one event than in the previous three years combined roasting and selling coffee.

That was one of the reasons (among many) I sold my coffee roasting company. No, I'm not saying roasting coffee isn't a viable option for a startup. Besides, I already wrote a whole chapter on it. I could've easily put more into it to make a legitimate go of it if I wanted to. But for me, it was the realization that as much as my imposter syndrome told me, I was a content matter expert. Not only that, but I should lean into it more. And I did.

I will ask you the question again … what are you good at? In what areas are you an expert?

Sure, none of us are "top-level" experts in our fields, but that's ok. Just because we're not the best at something, we're any less valuable. Is LeBron James any less of a player because he's not Michael Jordan? (I'm of the persuasion LeBron is better than Michael, but that's for another conversation.)

So then the question becomes, how do we turn our expertise into a way to earn a living? To me, that's the most critical question. It's one thing to get over imposter syndrome, but a whole different thing to begin towards building a startup that revolves around you and your expertise. That does sound intimidating, but it doesn't have to.

Recently I had coffee with a mid-20s YouTuber. When I say YouTuber, I'm talking about someone who's only been at it for 3-4 months. However, already he has 3,000 subscribers and is making $1,000 a month through paid advertisers and sponsors. Wait, what? That fast? He must be some sage expert on something significant, right?

Truth be told, he streams and provides commentary and instructional videos about some new game I never even heard of. It's a card game similar to Magic the Gathering but played online. Not only that, but he also talks about cryptocurrencies and NFTs. That's it. He, too, was shocked it had been taking off so fast. He started it as something fun when he had a full-time job but was laid off. Because of growth and momentum, he decided to go for it and tackle it hard.

See? He's an expert voice in a new game most have never heard of. He's monetizing it off YouTube because that's where his target audience is at. Your topic and target audience may mean you're speaking at brewpubs or lecture halls or on Tik Tok and not YouTube. That's the point. It's not as much about what the platform is as much as who you are, what your expertise is in, and where your target audience is at. That is the magic formula.

Here's a fun exercise: come up with a list of 3-5 topics you're growing towards becoming an expert in. On the same paper (or app), begin defining not only who your target audience is but where they are. The where could be both geographic and what social media platforms they're on. Then your rough strategy is to: (1) clarify your message, (2) determine the most effective means of teaching and getting your content out, and (3) start branding and promoting towards that end. While that may be an oversimplification, it's more than enough to get started.

What is holding you back?

CHAPTER 10

PRODUCT REVIEWER

For some, a product reviewer may be synonymous with being a YouTuber or influencer. While that is true, it's not the whole story. Simply typing out the title "Product Reviewer" can send us off in myriad directions. So what do I mean by a product reviewer? Not only that but how can one earn a living or at least side-hustle income from it?

But it all has to start somewhere, right? Case in point (and perfect timing), just this morning, a coffee roasting company hit me up on my @nachothevan Instagram. They DM'd me, told me they love my photos and asked if they could send me free coffee. Wait, did someone mention "free coffee?" So my response was, "Of course!" (Truth be told, at the time of writing this sentence, I only have 182 followers on my Nacho IG account. It's not a prominent account.)

Here's what will happen ... I'll get their coffee, drink it at home, take it into my van, snap a few photos, and give a shoutout post. That's it. Simple. And last weekend, I did just that. I had a blast.

Now, did I get paid? Was I offered any financial compensation? The answer to both was "no." But make no mistake, this little exercise will inevitably launch me (or I should say @nachothevan) into probably receiving more products related to all-things van life, coffee, etc. Is this what I want? Something I want to pursue? Do I want to make a career of this or at least some side-hustle money?

While, again, my answer is "no," I'll never close the doors for future opportunities. But for a moment, let's pretend that this is something I am interested in pursuing. What would I do next? Where do I go from here?

Well, a simple solution would be that in addition to doing some photos and a shoutout post on Instagram, what if I also videoed me brewing a cup of their coffee and drinking it? Not only that, but I talk through my process … how I'm choosing to brew this cup while sitting inside Nacho the MTB Van, what one needs to brew coffee inside a van, considerations for brewing on the road, and then talking about the coffee itself. That's easily a 3-5 minute video.

Inevitably, someone or some company will see that. If I do a great job and get a positive response, they may reach out to me about reviewing one of their products. Maybe it's an electric power source for running electronics inside my van this time. It could be a new pourover dripper from a new company, a new Bluetooth scale that runs from an iPhone app, a new compact electric or manual coffee grinder, or another coffee roasting company.

All of a sudden, as I continue to get products, I'm creating content both for video as well as taking photos. Not only that, but I could add to my website or create a whole new website dedicated to product reviews. In it, I'm also writing articles and using social media to point people to my website and my affiliate links so I can get paid when people buy products on Amazon (or wherever) since they're using my links.

Wait, why am I not doing this?

Now you can see how it all works ... or could work. We often think of a product reviewer or influencer as a 20-something female who jet-sets worldwide, staying in luxury villas and doing photoshoots for fashion companies. It certainly is that ... and the tow truck driver in Alaska who's reviewing an electric jump starter kit. That last example came to mind when I wanted to buy an electric jump starter kit for my van. I read reviews but ultimately was sold by watching YouTube reviews of some dude in the winter in Alaska jump-starting cars that had sat dead in his lot. In other words, anyone can do product reviews.

Last year I taught an undergrad course called Social Media and Analytics. I read anything I could get my hands on related to social media in preparation. I plowed through a stack of books that ranged from textbooks to one of my favorite books, *Influencer: Building Your Personal Brand in the Age of Social Media* by Brittany Hennessy. While I didn't use it for my class, it was an incredible book to read and consider.

She wrote the book seemingly for that 20-something young woman who's trying to make a go of it as a content creator and influencer. Her day job is connecting brands with influencers. Throughout the book, she gives many practical tips ranging from expectations to navigating contracts. Also, a gem is that in each chapter, she interviews influencers and has them share their stories. There's one quote from the book I'd like to share.

At the end of chapter 4, one of the influencers (Joy Cho) shares some great advice:

> My biggest advice for anyone with a similar goal [becoming an influencer] is to keep putting yourself out there and show work that you want to be making (even if no one is hiring you to do that work yet). I think the biggest misconception is that these things fell into my lap, and that's not true. Ninety percent of the bigger projects I've worked on were from me reaching out and pitching my work and ideas to a brand.[1]

Did you read that? Ninety percent was from her reaching out to potential brands and clients. You see, it's not about sitting back and simply waiting. Those who're successful at this actually treat it as a legitimate business, hustle

---

[1] Hennessy, *Influencer*, 126.

hard, and persist. You'll often get no after no … until you hit that yes.

Hopefully, my little example and thought experiment revealed to you that you can be a product reviewer … and dare I say "influencer?" It's there for the taking. The cost? Time, effort, and rejection. But those who persevere can make a go of it.

WRAP-UP

Ten startup ideas that cost little to no upfront money to start. The goal wasn't to create an exhaustive list. Besides, it was only ten ideas. The hope is for a spark. Your spark. An idea. A-ha moment. Something that gets your creative juices flowing and thoughts swirling around in your imagination. If so, mission accomplished.

I also want to encourage you. Put away self-doubt and negative thinking. Uninvite imposter syndrome from your life. You can do this. One step at a time. You got this. I believe in you.

ABOUT THE AUTHOR

Sean Benesh lives in Portland, Oregon working in higher education and mentoring and coaching startup entrepreneurs.

NEED HELPING GETTING YOUR STARTUP IDEA OFF THE GROUND?

LEARN MORE ABOUT OUR STARTUP COACHING.

ABOUT STARTUP COACHING

At URTHTREK, we work with all sorts of people striving to launch their businesses or non-profits from scratch. While the motives for launching a startup are varied, this gets to the heart of a more profound need. We all want to be part of something that gives our life meaning and purpose. For those we've coached, that is what they're looking for in their startup journey.

To launch a startup from scratch, you need someone you can trust to walk you through the process from idea to launch.

When it comes to startups, we feel overwhelmed, intimidated, and don't even know where to start. Don't let fear and ambiguity come between you and your dream. In case you're wondering, we were in the same boat with you at one time. Overwhelmed. Intimidated.

That's why we created a personalized one-on-one coaching program to guide you through making your startup dream a reality. Here's how it works:

STEP 1 - Sign up for startup coaching.

STEP 2 - We'll teach and help you start and grow a business or non-profit.

STEP 3 - Enjoy the freedom of doing something that you're good at, interested in, and passionate about.

"THE COACHING EXPERIENCE WAS INCREDIBLE. I STARTED OFF NOT SURE WHAT I WANTED TO START. BY THE TIME I FINISHED I HAD A GROWING BRAND THAT I LAUNCHED FROM SCRATCH."

SAM WAKE, FOUNDER OF KIDS & COBRAS

ABOUT URTHTREK

Many would-be entrepreneurs struggle to land on a startup idea and know-how to launch a brand. We offer a curriculum and provide a coach who walks you through the process so you can launch a startup where you enjoy the freedom of doing something that you're good at, interested in, and passionate about.

urthtrek.com
sean@urthtrek.com
@urthtrek